EXCLAMATIONS OF

THanKs!

*Prayers, Poems, and Bits of Encouragement
for Those Who Serve the Lord*

COMPILED BY GAIL MARSH

www.CTAinc.com

Exclamations of Thanks!
Compiled by Gail Marsh

Copyright © 2004 by CTA, Inc. 1625 Larkin Williams Rd., Fenton, MO 63026-1205

ISBN 0-9754499-9-0
Printed in Thailand

1 2 3 4 5 6 7 8 9 10   13 12 11 10 0

THanks!

Presented to

In appreciation for your service to the Lord!

From

Date

E *very time you cross my mind,*
I break out in exclamations of thanks to God.

Philippians 1:3 THE MESSAGE

Every calling is great
when greatly pursued.

Oliver Wendell Holmes Jr.

We are [God's] workmanship, created in Christ Jesus for good works,
which God prepared beforehand that we should walk in them.

Ephesians 2:10 NKJV

Every day, dear Father, work your grace in me.
Strengthened by your Spirit,
I'll serve you joyfully!

*P repare God's people
for works of service,
so that the body of Christ
may be built up
until we all reach unity in the faith
and in the knowledge
of the Son of God.*

Ephesians 4:12–13

A life without cause
is a life without effect.

Barbarella

You are a chosen people,
a royal priesthood,
a holy nation,
a people belonging to God,
that you may declare the praises of him
who called you out of darkness
into his wonderful light.

I Peter 2:9

A pessimist sees the difficulty
in every opportunity;
an optimist sees the opportunity
in every difficulty.

Winston Churchill

May thy rich grace impart
Strength to my fainting heart,
My zeal inspire!
As thou hast died for me,
Oh, may my love to thee
Pure, warm, and changeless be,
A living fire!

Ray Palmer

Do what you can,
with what you have,
where you are.

Theodore Roosevelt

God
shall supply all your need
according to His riches in glory
by Christ Jesus.

Philippians 4:19 NKJV

It's kind of fun
to do the impossible.

Walt Disney

Coming together is the beginning.
Keeping together is progress.
Working together is success.

Henry Ford

---

*Make every effort
to keep the unity of the Spirit
through the bond of peace.
There is one body and one Spirit—
just as you were called to one hope
when you were called—
one Lord,
one faith,
one baptism;
one God and Father of all,
who is over all
and through all
and in all.*

Ephesians 4:3–6

Stayed upon Jehovah,
Hearts are fully blest;
Finding, as he promised,
Perfect peace and rest.

Frances R. Havergal

Thus says the LORD:
"I will extend peace . . .
like a river."

Isaiah 66:12 NKJV

Heavenly Father,
help me remember to rely on you;
to place my acts of service into your hands;
and, in peace, to await your blessings.

Never let a bump in the road derail heaven-inspired plans.

Now to Him
who is able to keep you from stumbling,
And to present you faultless
Before the presence of His glory
with exceeding joy,
To God our Savior,
Who alone is wise,
Be glory and majesty,
Dominion and power,
Both now and forever.

Jude 24–25 NKJV

Serve others with eagerness.
It will make your heart dance!

You have not lived today
until you have done something
for someone
who can never repay you.

John Bunyon

Direct, control, suggest, this day,
All I design or do or say
That all my powers, with all their might,
In thy sole glory may unite.

Thomas Ken

Seek the LORD and His strength;
seek His face evermore.
Psalm 105:4 NKJV

Today Lord,
keep my eyes
steadily focused on you.
Amen.

God answers knee mail.

If any of you lacks wisdom,
he should ask God,
who gives generously to all
without finding fault,
and it will be given to him.
But when he asks, he must believe.

James 1:6

I am trusting thee, Lord Jesus;
Never let me fall.
I am trusting thee forever
And for all.

Frances R. Havergal

Rest
is the sweet sauce
of labor.

Plutarch

Dear Savior Jesus,
As I rest, renew my zeal for you.
Help me, dear Lord, to sleep in peace
and wake refreshed, renewed.

[God]
gives His beloved
sleep.
Psalm 127:2 NKJV

THanKs!

The LORD has done
great things for us,
and we are filled with joy.
Psalm 126:3

In the garden of your life
grow a grateful heart.

Now thanks be to God
who always leads us in triumph in Christ,
and through us
diffuses the fragrance of His knowledge
in every place.
2 Corinthians 2:14 NKJV

We make a living by what we get;
we make a life by what we give.
Winston Churchill

God . . . saved us and called us to a holy life.
2 Timothy 1:8–9

Give me a faithful heart,
Likeness to thee,
That each departing day henceforth may see
Some work of love begun,
Some deed of kindness done,
Some wanderer sought and won,
Something for thee.
S. D. Phelps

You cannot kindle a fire
in any other heart
until it is burning
in your own.

Anonymous

Let the word of Christ dwell in you richly . . .
teaching and admonishing one another in psalms
and hymns and spiritual songs,
singing with grace
in your hearts to the Lord.

Colossians 3:16 NKJV

Draw me to your Word,
dear Father, every day.
Speak your truth and strengthen me
along life's way.

All things are difficult
before they are easy.

Thomas Fuller

Never give up!
For this [may be] just the place and time
that the tide will turn.

Harriet Beecher Stowe

Wait on the LORD;
Be of good courage,
And He shall strengthen your heart;
Wait, I say, on the LORD!
Psalm 27:14 NKJV

Character
may be manifested
in the great moments,
but it is made
in the small ones.

Phillip Brooks

The King will reply,
"I tell you the truth,
whatever you did
for one of the least of these brothers of mine,
you did for me."

Matthew 25:40

The smallest jobs demand the biggest hearts.

With Jesus,
it's easier to see the world
sunny-side up!

Whatever is true,
whatever is noble,
whatever is right,
whatever is pure,
whatever is lovely,
whatever is admirable—
if anything is excellent or praiseworthy—
think about such things.
Whatever you have learned or received
or heard from me,
or seen in me—put it into practice.
And the God of peace
will be with you.
Philippians 4:8–9

Give generously . . .
and do so without a grudging heart;
then because of this
the LORD your God
will bless you
in all your work
and in everything
you put your hand to.
Deuteronomy 15:10

A person starts to live
when he can live
outside himself.

Albert Einstein

O God of mercy, God of light,
In love and mercy infinite,
Teach us, as ever in your sight,
To live our lives in you.
Teach us the lesson Jesus taught:
To feel for those his blood has bought,
That every deed and word and thought
May work a work for you.

Godfrey Thring

Do not seek greatness.
Seek to be humble.

Anonymous

---

*[God] guides the humble
in what is right
and teaches them his way.*
Psalm 25:9

---

*Be completely humble and gentle;
be patient,
bearing with one another
in love.*
Ephesians 4:2

Do not go where the path may lead;
go instead where there is no path
and leave a trail.

Ralph Waldo Emerson

---

*Now I urge you
to keep up your courage.*
Acts 27:22

Whoever loves much, does much.

Thomas à Kempis

He who is filled
with love and hope
is filled with God himself.

St. Augustine

Draw me into your Word, Lord.
Help me to meet you there.
That strengthened by your gentleness,
Your love and hope I'll share.

The eyes of the LORD
are on those who fear him,
on those whose hope
is in his unfailing love.
Psalm 33:18

To all who received [Christ],
to those who believed in his name,
he gave the right to become children of God.
John 1:12

God is the Father
who kisses our offenses
into everlasting forgiveness.

Henry Ward Beecher (adapted)

*I press on
toward the goal
to win the prize
for which God has called me
heavenward
in Christ Jesus.*
Philippians 3:14

So long as we love we serve.

Robert Louis Stevenson

Whatever you do,
work at it with all your heart,
as working for the Lord,
not for men,
since you know
that you will receive
an inheritance from the Lord
as a reward.
It is the Lord Christ
you are serving.
Colossians 3:23–24

THanks!

Freely we serve,
because we freely love.

John Milton

Let brotherly love continue.

Hebrews 13:1 NKJV

There's no such thing
as an insignificant act
of service.

Lord,
help me to reflect your grace
every day, in every place.
Amen.

You serve the Lord Christ.
Colossians 3:24 NKJV

Service . . .
Giving what you don't have to give.
Giving when you don't need to give.
Giving because you want to give.

Damien Hess

As servants of Christ,
[do] the will of God
from the heart.
Ephesians 6:6 NKJV

Serve the LORD . . .
And rejoice.
Psalm 2:11 NKJV

One drop of water
helps to swell the ocean.
A spark of fire
helps give light to the world.
No act of service is too small.

H. More

Dear Father,
Thank you for your gifts
of talent, time, and grace.
In all I do,
in all I say,
help others see your face.
Amen.

Love . . .
endures all things.
1 Corinthians 13:4–7 NKJV

May the God
who gives endurance and encouragement
give you a spirit of unity among yourselves
as you follow Christ Jesus.
Romans 15:5

C hrist didn't promise a smooth road of service.
He promised to walk that road with you.

Anonymous

The eternal God is your refuge,
And underneath are the everlasting arms.
Deuteronomy 33:27 NKJV

There are two days in the week
about which I never worry.
Two carefree days
kept sacredly free
from fear and apprehension.
One of these days is Yesterday.
And the other day I do not worry about
is Tomorrow.

Robert Jones Burdette

---

*May the God of hope
fill you with all joy and peace
as you trust in him,
so that you may overflow with hope
by the power of the Holy Spirit.*

Romans 15:13

He has half the deed done
who has made
a beginning.

Horace

Be ready to do the work of the LORD.
Numbers 8:11

Heavenly Father,
Inspire and encourage me,
From hesitancy set me free.
Urge me ever onward go
For heaven's service here below.
Amen.

We are weaving the future
on the loom
of today.

Grace Dawson

"Your work will be rewarded,"
declares the LORD. . . .
"There is hope for your future."
Jeremiah 31:16–17

He who calls you is faithful.
1 Thessalonians 5:24 NKJV

If you have love in your heart,
you will always
have something
to give.

Anonymous

True service
is love
in action.

We always thank God for . . .
your labor prompted by love.
1 Thessalonians 1:2—3

When you begin the day,
O, never fail to say;
May Jesus Christ be praised!
And at your work rejoice
To sing with heart and voice,
May Jesus Christ be praised!

German hymn

He who glories,
let him glory in the LORD.
1 Corinthians 1:31 NKJV

Thank you, Jesus,
for allowing me to serve you.
Amen.

A servant's hands
may never know
whose life
they touch.

Anonymous

Let brotherly love continue.
Do not forget to entertain strangers,
for by so doing
some have unwittingly
entertained angels.
Hebrews 13:1–2 NKJV

Through love serve one another.
Galatians 5:13 NKJV

Actions
speak louder
than words;
let your words
teach
and your actions
speak.

St. Anthony of Padua

---

*Blessed are the dead
who die in the Lord. . . .
They will rest
from their labor,
for their deeds
will follow them.*

Revelation 14:13

Start
by doing what's necessary,
then what's possible,
and suddenly
you are doing
the impossible.

St. Francis of Assisi

---

*For with God
nothing will be impossible.*
Luke 1:37 NKJV

When I can't,
God can.
Anonymous

44

Strong in the Lord of hosts
And in his mighty power.
Who in the strength of Jesus trusts
Is more than conqueror.

Charles Wesley

---

*Be strong
in the Lord
and in the power
of His might.*
Ephesians 6:10 NKJV

---

*We are more than conquerors
through him who loved us.*
Romans 8:37

The smallest good deed
is better than
the grandest intention.

Anonymous

---

*[God] will not forget your work
and the love you have shown him
as you have helped his people
and continue to help them.*

Hebrews 6:10

It is always
a privilege to serve.

The harvest is plentiful
but the workers are few.
Ask the Lord of the harvest, therefore,
to send out workers
into his harvest field.
Matthew 9:37–38

Go into all the world and
preach the Gospel.
If necessary, use words.

St. Francis of Assisi

If anyone serves,
he should do it
with the strength God provides,
so that in all things
God may be praised
through Jesus Christ.
To him be the glory and the power
for ever and ever.
1 Peter 4:11

Lord Jesus, let your power move
Within my heart, and help me love
That I may serve you more each day,
And trust in you to guide my way.
Amen.